BRIAN GITACHU

Story Time With Brian

a Collection

Brian Gitachu

for Art Tay. I miss you, bro.

Contents

Preface

This book is what happens when you have wild experiences in life.

I love telling stories. When I'm around friends, I can sit and tell stories for hours on end. My friends wouldn't believe some of the stories that I would tell them, they thought I was making them up. When I would tell them it was true, they would shake their heads in disbelief.

Eventually, I decided to start chronicling some of my mishaps (and random thoughts) for the purpose of publishing a book. I write almost everyday and there's no reason that I shouldn't create something. That's how *Story Time With Brian: a Collection* came about.

I didn't have a "central theme" when I was putting this book together. I just wanted to put together a few of my favorite writings to share with people who may or may not find my life adventures interesting and/or humorous.

Every story in this book is true. On a few occasions, I will change the names, but aside from a small name change or two, this entire book is a work of nonfiction.

I hope you enjoy reading this book as much as I enjoyed writing it. Writing is my therapy, and if reading is your therapy, hopefully we can help each other out.

What follows are stories that make my friends think I'm crazy. I don't mind.

Enjoy.

Acknowledgement

I want to dedicate this space to some very important people who I appreciate and want to thank, in no particular order. *Johnetta Gitachu, John Gitachu, Brandon Sullivan, Brenton Sullivan, Braxton Call, Isaiah Sullivan, Krista Sullivan, Esther "Cheri" Njeri Mwaura, Faith Wambui Mwaura, Michele Brown, Ronnie Brown Sr., Ronnie Brown Jr., Ronnie Brown III, Alexis Brown, Kenneth Crume Sr., Kenneth Crume Jr., Sharonda Robinson, Daron Robinson Sr., Daron Robinson Jr., Donnie Robinson, Robert "KC Chef" Andrade, Mimi Davis, Sean Mitchell, Robert Jefferson, Kennia Barnes, Latisha Fletcher, Lindsey Jackson, Brandy Famuliner, Atlanta Nicole, Chanell Ellis, Darryl Johnson Jr., mama Brenda, Jo Jo, Midknight, Randall Jackson, Franklin Jackson, Beverly Sullivan-Brown.*
A special shout out to Damon Lee Patterson and Tee Ervin for constantly telling me to write a book. Here we go, gentlemen.
For Art Tay. I love you, bro.

My Mama Said

My mother and I, 2020.

I love my mama.

My mama is one of the funniest people I've had the privilege of being around. On top of her being funny, she's smart, makes the world's greatest fried chicken, and has a photogenic memory.

She's also the worst person to help you with your school work.

I was in the first grade and we were working on a Columbus Day project. Mrs. Whitman told us this story of how this Christopher Columbus character was looking for India but ended up in America and that's why the Natives are called "Indians." Being the naive, imaginative kid that I was, I thought the man was an adventurer and I fucking *LOVE* adventures and adventurers! He was cool in my book.

Until I went home.

I got to the house and I had my stuff sprawled all over the place, getting ready to make this epic project and then my mom walked in.

"Boy! What the hell are you doing with all this shit in my living room? You better get this cleaned up!"

I told her, "Mom, I'm working on this project for school. Did you know Christopher Columbus, a famous adventurer, discovered America and named the Indians 'Indians'?" I felt like I just taught my mama something new and it was a glorious feeling.

Short-lived, but glorious.

"Son, everything you just said was wrong. For one, that mothafucka ain't no 'adventurer'. He was a *stupid mothafucka who got lost.* He was supposed to go to India, but his dumb ass ended up in the Americas where there were *MILLIONS* of people already here. And they're not called 'Indians,' they're

Native Americans! Not only that, he came over here with them dirty ass germs and made the Natives sick and a lot of them died. *Fuck Christopher Columbus.*"

Damn. I thought the dude was a super cool adventurer guy. That revelation completely changed the way I looked at Columbus. I hated him now. He was a fraud.

I went back to school and it was time to present our assignments to the class. Everyone else had dioramas and pictures and shit; all giddy about this faux adventurer. I sat there disgusted in my classmates. I'm the only non-white kid in class and I'm the only one who knew this 'adventurer' was the fucking outbreak monkey? I couldn't wait for my turn.

Mrs. Whitman finally calls my name and I get in front of the class and let them have it!

I told the class, "Christopher Columbus didn't discover *anything!* People were already living in the United States! You can't discover a place where people are already living! He also killed a bunch of people because he was dirty and he probably had the cooties! Or AIDS!"

My classmates sat there in a state of shock. Mrs. Whitman, who was already accustomed to my bullshit, sat at her desk shaking her head, preparing to do damage control on the crushed dreams of future wannabe 'adventurers'.

"Christopher Columbus didn't have the cooties! You take that back!" yelled one classmate.

"He *DID* discover America! My mommy said he's a hero!" said the girl who ate glue.

While I was standing in front of the class telling all my classmates that their parents - and in essence, Mrs. Whitman, who we loved - lied to them, Mrs. Whitman finally got up from her seat and regained control of class. She immediately

3

switched subjects from Columbus having cooties (or AIDS) to chocolate chip cookies. My classmates lost their shit over the cookies, forgetting all about Christopher Columbus in that instance! I ate my cookies alone in the corner because fuck those other kids and fuck Christopher Columbus!

After class, Mrs. Whitman stopped me from leaving to have a talk.

"Brian, you're an extremely intelligent little boy. Everything you said in your presentation was correct and your mother taught you well. But next time, let me look at your assignment beforehand so we can make sure it doesn't cause a scene in class again, ok?"

"Ok, Mrs. Whitman."

"One more thing, Brian."

"Yes?"

"Please don't tell these kids in December that your mother told you Santa Claus isn't real."

Damn, I can never have any fun.

Me and Mrs. Jones

Baby Brian, 1986 or '87.

In school, I was blessed to have been taught by two *really* wonderful Black teachers: Mrs. Thelma Jones at Franklin Elementary in Wichita, Kansas and Mrs. Dora Boyd-Love at Troost Elementary and Westport Middle School in Kansas City, Missouri. This is about Mrs. Jones.

I was the "token" Black student in Mrs. Jones' second grade class at a predominantly white school and felt alone. Mrs. Jones went above and beyond to make me feel welcomed and to constantly remind me that I was just as smart as any of my classmates.

The school was going to put on a production of *The Nutcracker* and I decided to audition. I practiced for the audition for a week, an audition I did really well in. When the parts were cast, I was devastated to see that I didn't get one. Mrs. Jones, seeing how devastated I was, told me, "Brian, I'm going to put you in the next play."

She knew I was hurt from not getting a part in the school play, so she let me skip the assembly, knowing I had no interest in being in attendance. I stayed in her classroom to draw and color while the rest of the school was in the auditorium.

A few months later, Mrs. Jones made good on her promise. She was in charge of the next school play and guess who got the starring role? **BRIAN!** The little Black kid who was made to feel as though he wasn't "good enough" for *The Nutcracker* was going to be the main attraction! I may have had just three lines, but I was undoubtedly the star of the production. Mrs. Jones and I stayed after school for a week or so making a Jayhawk costume from construction paper. She was *very* dedicated to me getting a chance to shine on the stage! Together we made the most glorious Jayhawk costume this side of Kansas University.

I worked my ass off studying my three lines because Mrs.

Jones was so dedicated to me and I refused to let her down. She was not only dedicated to my education, but also dedicated to my self-esteem, self-worth, and most of all, my happiness. She never let me feel down about myself or let me feel like I was "less than" any other student.

The day of the play arrives and everything goes as planned... until I get on stage. Once on stage, the entire audience starts laughing at me! I looked down and noticed that my costume was backwards! I was so embarrassed, I almost started crying. That's when I heard Mrs. Jones from the crowd yell *"GO FOR IT, BRIAN!"* She had more faith in me than almost any other person I've ever known in my entire life. I was able to confidently recite my lines over the laughter and when I was done, Mrs. Jones was whistling and giving me a standing ovation. The staff and the parents followed suit. It was one of the greatest days of my life.

My family moved to Kansas City, Missouri when I was in the fourth grade. I never forgot how much love and confidence Mrs. Jones instilled in me - an afraid, alone, shy little Black kid. She made me believe in myself and in my talents. She taught me that I could do anything I put my mind to. I still believe it thirty-plus years later.

I would be the "token" Black student once again years later at an Arizona community college. Thanks to Mrs. Thelma Jones I was no longer afraid of being the only Black student. I was confident in the knowledge that I was just as smart, worthy, and capable as every other student thanks to a second grade teacher in Wichita, Kansas who changed my life and the way I looked at it.

Mrs. Thelma Jones was one of the greatest educators I've ever been around. Hats off to her.

7

Brian the R&B Singer

Little baby Brian, 1986.

If you know anything about me, then you know I love music. When I was a young pup, I had dreams of being an R&B singer. Not just ANY R&B singer, but the deep-voiced guy from Boyz II Men.

I thought that dude was the coolest dude on the planet! He was a singer, he had a voice that melted the panties off of women, and he had a cane. At that time in my life, I thought only pimps had canes and I thought pimps were cool - don't judge me. Another thing I liked about the deep-voiced guy was the fact that all he did was apologize on songs! Being the world-class screw up that I am, I can apologize with the best of them! *This is easy money, champ!*

So here I am in the sixth grade and the school talent show is on the horizon. Here's my chance to show the world (which at that time consisted of my Westport Middle School peers, the staff, and my parents) that I am going to be the NEW deep-voiced guy in Boyz II Men. The gym teacher was in charge of selecting the talent, so during gym class I asked to sign up for the talent show. The gym teacher asks, "What are you going to do?" As confidently as I could, I told her, "Blow the roof off this joint with these golden vocals." She gave me the side-eye! I thought to myself, *"Okay, gym teacher, you'll be the main lady throwing their panties on stage once I'm famous."*

Around this time, puberty was kicking my ass. My hair was growing in weird places, I'm staring at breasts more than usual, my voice was cracking, my face was breaking out - I was miserable. I was thinking my voice was going to develop into this deep, silky, seductive, baritone voice. I truly believed I was well on my way to becoming a deep-voiced R&B singer dude! I went as far as going to the thrift store to look for a cane! I was fully invested in my R&B dreams. Nothing could stop me.

9

The day of the talent show audition, I decided to wear a suit. It was an oversized, cherry red Montgomery Ward monstrosity that sat in a closet at my dad's apartment almost all of my sixth grade year. I got a fresh haircut for the audition, I wore Old Spice aftershave for the ladies - I was ready to put on a show! You couldn't convince me that I wasn't a star!

Being an overly confident potential superstar, I decided to sing "For The Cool In You" by Babyface. Smooth, right?

Well, there was one small detail I failed to mention: I couldn't sing. At all.

As smart as I've been told I am, small details befuddle me at times - such as actually practicing and attempting to sing. You see, I told myself that I wanted to be the deep-voiced guy when I was around six years old. Not once did I take a singing lesson or practice or *anything*. I just assumed once my voice was deep, I'd be a natural singer. I probably didn't sing one song between the first and sixth grade. Hell, I didn't even practice the song I chose for the talent show!

We were in the auditorium for the audition and I'm far too confident. I look at the other kids auditioning and I'm thinking, "Amateurs, behold! You're in the presence of a future Grammy Award winning, multi-platinum, deep-voiced R&B dude! Pay homage, peasants!" I hear my last name being butchered, so I guess that's my cue. I proceed to center stage to manifest my destiny! The gym teacher cues the tape and I give it everything I have.

I'm maybe twenty to thirty seconds into the song and it's becoming apparent that singing *IS NOT* my calling. I was not destined to be a singer. I sounded terrible. I didn't even recognize my own voice!

The gym teacher - bless her sweet soul - pulled me to the

side after four of THE longest minutes of my life and said to me, "Brian, you're smart, you're funny, you're the reason I read the school newspaper. You're an absolute *treasure*! But dear, singing is not for you. Let me reiterate: **YOU ARE NOT A GOOD SINGER.** But since you're *so damn adorable in your widdle bitty suit wooking wike a widdle bitty man*, I'll let you walk the runway with the models."

Yes, she talked to me like I was a baby… right there in front of my "Beginning of Puberty" mustache.

Mentally, I'm still processing the laughs I heard onstage and was working to identify the *infidels* responsible, but I heard what she was saying loud and clear.

With my heart broken in a million pieces, I asked her, "So I'll never be the deep-voiced guy in Boyz II Men?"

She laughed in my face, ya'll.

I said aloud "***Ain't this a bitch?!***" and stormed off. I had no intention of "strutting my stuff on the catwalk; doing my little turn around on the catwalk." I didn't even go to school the day of the talent show.

The Dream was over.

To make matters worse, the gym teacher gave me a **B** in gym for saying "Ain't this a bitch!" and I ended the semester with a 3.9 instead of a 4.0.

She not only crushed my R&B dreams, but my dream of a perfect grade point average, as well!

On the bright side, she *did* encourage me to write more, so I guess I followed the right dream, right?

Right?

Nah, I should be in Boyz II Men. She was just hating.

Brian Joins the Choir

Brian in Kenya, 1995.

You would think after performing so horribly at the audition for the sixth grade talent show that I would leave music alone. Well, you're wrong.

In the seventh grade, I transferred to Lincoln College Prep Academy, the best school in the district in regards to academics. On the first day of classes, I received my schedule and saw that I had a choir class. I'm excited again - maybe my R&B dreams weren't dead! Maybe the universe wanted me to actually *practice* and become the superstar that I was destined to be! I wait to prove my sixth grade gym teacher wrong!

Unfortunately for me, this choir class was nothing like I imagined it. Did you know this choir teacher had the *audacity* to make us actually *read* sheet music? *Hold on, lady* - I'm only here to work on becoming the deep-voiced guy in Boyz II Men, not some pianist or cellist! Besides, the deep-voiced guy only apologized and walked with a cane like a pimp! Do I look like I'm here to READ MUSIC?

No way!

Get the hell out of here!

I guess it goes without saying I didn't do well in that class at the beginning.

A few months in, we were finally singing and honestly, I still sounded terrible. My voice *still* hasn't become silky and seductive. I was shook! Considering there were approximately twenty-five or thirty students in the class, I decided to hide my voice. I'm thinking I should be good for a while and no one will hear my singing voice until it's ready, that way I can preserve the golden pipes and my confidence stays intact.

Well, this choir wasn't the average seventh grade choir. We were a *traveling* choir! Once it got close to Christmas season, the choir teacher began passing out Christmas music for us to get familiar with because we were taking the show on the road: nursing homes, shopping centers, anywhere people wanted to listen to seventh grade carolers, we were there.

Being short my entire life afforded me a front row spot in the choir. At the time, I knew I was up front because I was smaller than everyone else, yet my huge ego refused to acknowledge it. My ego thought "Brian, *YOU* are the star of this show! You need to let them know who's the future deep-voiced guy in Boyz II Men!"

That was a terrible decision.

December rolls around and I'm still not singing loud enough to be heard. Yet, in my brain, the applause we receive after performing is all for me! I'm thinking to myself, *"They love me! They recognize my greatness!"* I decided it's time to give the fans their money's worth!

(They were free shows, but that's really no one's business.)

I started hamming it up, you guys.

Big time.

Remember how I said I was hiding my voice? Dude, I was *lip-syncing*! I figured if Milli Vanilli could get away with it, so could I! The fact that I learned all the words to all the songs that we sang that year helped me out significantly in the credibility department. I refused to actually sing - I was letting those *amateurs* in class with me get a little shine before I was off to Motown Records.

We're not ALL meant to be R&B singers, you know?

That's show business.

I soon decided that I was going to start putting on a show so I became increasingly more demonstrative during rehearsals and performances. I would pretend to hit all these high notes - my eyes would be closed, my head would be tilted back, and my

14

mouth would be fully agape as if the voice of Teddy Pendergrass was going to magically manifest itself in my disappointing singing voice.

It was quite impressive for a seventh grade lip-synching performance.

The hating-ass choir teacher didn't think it was. She thought I was trying to embarrass my classmates. She was wrong: how could I embarrass *amateurs* who were clearly not on my potential *multi-platinum* level? C'mon, man! Anyway, she was none too happy that I was hamming it up and stopped rehearsal one day.

"Mr. Gitachu, what the hell are you doing?"

I answered as any superstar of my caliber would answer.

"Absolutely killing it with the 'Star Spangled Banner'. I'm doing the United States of America a favor, ma'am. You, this class, this country - you guys are forever indebted to me and my patriotism. *You're welcome.*"

She didn't like that answer. I knew she wouldn't because she couldn't see that I was manifesting my destiny. She was just another hater.

"Ok Mr. Gitachu, let's see what you can do."

She was putting me on the spot. The nerve of this simpleton choir teacher! How *dare* she attempt to embarrass ME? The *superstar* in the making? I guess she's gonna be another person I'm going to neglect to acknowledge on the rough and tumble road to fame and fortune.

I responded boldly, "What would you like for me to sing?"

"I want you to sing the national anthem in front of the entire class."

I wasn't worried. I had been hiding my voice for months so I figured it was maturing finely. Practicing at home in the mirror

15

and sounding good in the shower, I felt ready! I would not be deterred.

"O' say can you see…"

I was stopped dead in my tracks.

"Whatever you were doing before, continue doing *that* because singing is not what you're good at."

I was shocked! "So you don't want me to finish?!"

"*OF COURSE NOT*!" she laughed.

"But I know all the words! I promise!"

"I'm sure you do, Mr. Gitachu, but you're free to go back to lip-synching."

I was *devastated.* Another year, R&B superstardom foiled yet again. The fact I was given the green light to lip-sync didn't sit too well with me; I only did it because I thought I wasn't going to get caught. Getting caught *and* being told it was in the class' best interest to not sing was embarrassing. I took revenge by sabotaging choir class, singing at the top of my lungs. **YOU INFIDELS WERE GOING TO HEAR ME!** I only stopped sabotaging the class when I began to get written up and starting missing the field trips to go sing in public.

I went back to lip-syncing without the razzle-dazzle and star power I was accustomed to contributing.

Feeling defeated at the end of the school year - even with the very generous "B" I got in the class - I went to my counselor and told him to not put me in choir for the next school year.

"Why not?" he asked me. "You got a B!"

Determined not to let another person see me tuck my tail, I told him as egotistically as I could, *"Those amateurs aren't ready for me to bless them with the golden pipes!"*

"Whatever, Gitachu. Get to Latin class."

I walked out of his office feeling better. Maybe I didn't need choir - choir needed *ME!*

The dream would live to see another day!

My Mama's F

High school graduate Brian, 2002.

Home economics was one of my favorite classes in high school, mostly because we used to bake cookies at least twice a week. There were also cute girls in the class, *none* of which would talk to me, but it still counts as "a class full of cute girls." I even learned how to use a digital sewing machine. I was the Black male Martha Stewart.

Around the second semester of school, the home economics instructor began talking to the class about students going home with dolls! I was entirely too gangsta for that; I told Little Miss Home Ec Teacher, "*I ain't fucking playing with no doll, cuzz! You got me fucked up!*"

OK, that's a lie. I didn't say anything remotely close to that. It was more along the lines of, "I'm not going home with a baby doll, cuzz."

Yes, *I did* call my teachers "cuzz."

Well, the doll wasn't a regular doll. It was a "smart doll" or something. The little jerk cried, pooped, woke up in the middle of the night and all kinds of real baby person shit. I can't lie to you, it was a creepy looking, *Seed of Chucky* look alike.

Luckily for me, my high school was poor as hell and there weren't enough creepy looking babies to go around. I was relieved because I thought I got off the hook on the assignment. I went back to making my famous Stegosaurus-shaped raisin oatmeal cookies.

My famous Stegosaurus-shaped raisin oatmeal cookies were put on hiatus; Little Miss Home Ec Teacher had a substitute baby.

In lieu of a "smart baby," I received a five pound bag of flour in a diaper and a onesie.

I bullshit you not.

The assignment consisted of us having our "babies" for an entire week; making sure they're fed, dry, clean, not dead, etc.

Since I had a bag of flour in a diaper and a onesie, I just kept it in a plastic Aldi bag in my bedroom. I was not bringing a flour baby to school until it was time to return it.

That Thursday night, I walked into my mama's house to the greatest smell in the history of greatest smells: **MY MAMA'S FRIED CHICKEN!** I was *SUPER* excited - my mama makes the best fried chicken I have ever had in my entire life! Along with fried chicken, there were green beans, rice, cornbread, and red Kool Aid. I was in the midst of devouring my second plate of food when I remembered my mama saying something about not having flour the other day.

I ran to my room and the plastic Aldi bag was EMPTY! The only thing that remained was the onesie and the diaper. Fuck, I knew Flour Baby was a goner. I went to the kitchen and the once-five pound Flour Baby was half the original size and smelled of Lawry's Seasoned Salt.

I thought, "The hell with it - the school is going to get whatever Flour Baby I bring."

I got to school Friday and the home economics teacher was telling all the students with "smart babies" things like, "Good job!" and "It's not dead!" and things of that nature. I removed the Flour Baby from my backpack and Little Miss Home Ec Teacher said, "Brian, you can't just stuff babies in your pot-smelling backpack."

I thought to myself, *"How could she smell the weed from across the room?"*

Once the Flour Baby was removed from the plastic Aldi bag, the teacher said, "Brian, you can't just stuff babies in your pot-smelling Aldi bag in your pot-smelling backpack."

I thought to myself, "This lady must have a 'Go Go Gadget Nose' kind of nose or something!"

Then she saw my Flour Baby.

"WHAT THE HELL HAPPENED TO YOUR BABY? DID YOU NOT FEED THE BABY? HOW COULD YOU BE SO IRRESPONSIBLE?!?!"

Without hesitation, I interjected with, "First of all, you can't feed a flour baby. Second of all, and most importantly, my mama made fried chicken last night. So if you wanna give *ANYONE* an F, give it to my mama! She's downstairs in the cafeteria, making fried chicken *RIGHT NOW* for *THE ENTIRE SCHOOL!*"

My mom was one of the lunch ladies at my high school.

Somebody in the back of the class yelled out, "I'll donate my Flour Baby to the cause cuz yo' mama can cook like a mothafucka, cuzz!"

I still got an F, though, but that's my mama's F.

Love Thyself

Shocked and amazed Brian, 2020.

When I was younger, all I ever wanted to do was fit in. I wanted to be liked, accepted, and revered.

It didn't work.

I struggled with accepting the fact I was different from the people I was around. I would hang out with gangsters, but I was an honor roll student. I would hang out with honor roll students, but I was into gangster shit. I was too Kenyan for Black people and too Black for Kenyans. It was a terrible feeling.

I used to hide my interests and dumb myself down just for people to accept me. I usually love to laugh, crack jokes, and put a smile on someone's face, but all the girls I used to like would say, "Brian, you're too childish." I decided to try to change to impress the ladies and I spent a long time not laughing and joking as much. It was honestly one of the most depressing things I've endured.

I got into a situation where all of that changed. Without going into too much detail at this time, *all of the people I abandoned myself for abandoned me in the end.* I was heartbroken. I became someone I wasn't just to be friends with these people - but once the going got tough, they were gone.

I was depressed for a long time. Not only that, I felt like I was right back where I started: not knowing who I was.

I had to find Brian. Not only *find* Brian, but *embrace* and *love* Brian.

But which Brian?

Do I embrace the Brian that I became to attract friends? The street-running, police evading, serious-about-ignorance Brian who was ashamed of his intelligence? Ashamed of being kind of a dork? Ashamed to be Brian? Do I go back to being *that* Brian? The Brian the girls would talk to and the gangsters were cool with?

I couldn't do that to myself again.

In the end I realized I had to go back to being Brian. The *REAL* Brian. Let me tell you a few things about the *REAL* Brian that I've learned to love and that I find interesting:

I love to read and write. There's nothing in this world that I love more than being creative. While the friends that the fake Brian accumulated respected his ability as a person who could write raps, they didn't know that I wrote for the school newspaper from the 4th grade until my second semester of college, was a yearbook editor in high school, and wrote poetry. I'm a pretty ok writer.

I love outer space. It may seem like no surprise to people who know me now, but back in the day, I rarely talked about UFOs and space travel. I would be on the corner with the gangsters for hours on end, doing things that could get me sent to prison for a long time, and then go home to read "Secrets of the Universe." I was (and still am) a huge outer space geek who wishes to be abducted by aliens.

I'm very proud of my roots. I got teased a lot in high school about my last name. I was called every "African booty scratcher" in the book. I used to laugh it off, but to be honest, I was pissed off. I never understood why being a Kenyan was something people in class would make fun of. There was a time I used my mother's maiden name at school just to avoid getting teased for a while.

I eventually found out my last name was kind of unique.

Even in Kenya, you won't find a lot of people with my last name. Approximately eighty percent of the people I've contacted on social media who share my last name are my blood relatives. At one time, my mother and I was the only people in the state of Missouri with the last name "Gitachu." Another cool fact that I found out about my name is that *I'm the only Brian Gitachu in the history of the world* (as of this writing); that alone improved my self-esteem significantly.

I know exactly where my last name comes from and from whom. I've never felt more proud of my last name. The same people who teased me in school about it are now trying to get in touch with their "African roots" and abandoning their "slave names." It feels good that for me to get in touch with my roots and learn more about my family history, all I have to do is make a WhatsApp call.

I'm pretty funny sometimes. Had I known then what I know now, I wouldn't have been so eager to shed my sense of humor trying to impress teenage girls for the sake of late night phone conversations and breast fondling. There's nothing wrong with being "childish" at age seventeen - *you are a child!* One of my favorite things about myself is that I love to laugh and make people laugh.

As a person who has struggled my entire life with depression, I've noticed that the more I laugh and joke, the less I notice the sadness around me. I make jokes about anything. I have friends nowadays, ladies included, who call me now because they know that I'm available to make them smile.

I guess what I'm saying is stay true to yourself. Humans are fickle and if they don't like you, they just don't like you. There's nothing you can do to change that. You can commit felonies, use your mother's maiden name, hide all your science books from your drug dealing friends, and you still won't be loved or accepted. *Love and accept yourself and you'll attract the right people.*

Once I embraced being my *true* self, the type of friends I've made have changed tremendously. The people in my life now want what's best for me. They do things for me out of the kindness of their heart. They love and accept me at face value and don't want me to change anything positive that makes me who I am. If I like aliens, guess what? They're making alien jokes and telling me jokingly to not get abducted. They enjoy who I am and so do I, for a change.

Trust me: nobody in the world that you attempt to be is better than who you *really* are. Embrace your quirks. Embrace your uniqueness. **Embrace yourself first.**

Famous While Black

Big brother of the Groom Brian, 2018.

I don't want to be *famous* but I would love to be rich.

One of my goals is to write a best-selling book and to promote reading and creative writing of any genre in the inner city. I just don't want to be a celebrity. That shit seems terrible.

Especially while Black.

When former San Francisco 49ers quarterback Colin Kaepernick first began his peaceful protest during the playing of the national anthem, I would hear people say things like, "He's not oppressed; he was raised by a good White family!" All I could think was, *"What's that supposed to mean?"*

I find the whole argument hypocritical.

The same people who ask, "Where are all the Black leaders?" in times of crisis are the same people who parade athletes and entertainers around *as* our Black leaders. I'm not disrespecting the Black women and men who put their reputations and brands on the line at all, I'm just paraphrasing Malcolm X. Unfortunately for them, once these Black men and women take up the responsibility of being a Black leader wholeheartedly, the same people who propped them up as the leaders in our communities begin to tear them down and question their authenticity, their leadership, and the legitimacy of their respective messages due to their finances or their upbringing.

Here's the thing about people from financially stable backgrounds: those are some of the *main* people we need to take a stand. Just as it took some people who were never slaves to help free the slaves and just as it took some men to help women's suffrage, it's going to take some famous and well-established people to help those who are more vulnerable and struggling economically. People who want to genuinely help are always needed and welcomed, regardless of their financial background.

Does Colin Kaepernick being raised in a financially stable

white family take away from the legitimacy of his message? Absolutely not.

After a peaceful protest of a song that doesn't rhyme or have a dope beat or tell a great story or anything cool that I would like, people started dragging Kaepernick's name and reputation through the mud. Some people said they would never support the San Francisco 49ers ever again. Some were burning their Kaepernick jerseys and Nike products and posting it online. The comments left on Kaepernick's social media pages were outrageous.

He sacrificed a lot by taking a stand, rather you agree with what he stands for or not.

There are celebrities (who I won't name) that won't say a word: nothing constructive, consoling, soothing or anything that acknowledges the plight of people might who look like them and might share similar upbringings. Some of them are too busy ignoring the real world and are spending their free time "flexing" on social media and in these terrible music videos. On the occasions when they are directly confronted with questions about tough subjects like racial injustice and police brutality, they will show they are more or less disinterested. The late, great Tupac Shakur warned us about these kinds of celebrities before he was murdered.

(Speaking of music videos, ever since AJ & Free left BET's *106th and Park*, music videos have sucked. But that's just *my* opinion).

I would hate to be famous. I would hate walking on eggshells for a company who is bold enough to hire a Black face but remain silent and/or indifferent about Black issues in America. It would be unfortunate to work so hard on a craft, climb the ladder, kiss an *obscene* amount of ass and endure an *unfathomable* amount of bullshit and find that being famous doesn't shield you from being Black and being judged different when speaking on Black issues. Bad things can happen as soon as a celebrity opens their mouth to speak.

Almost immediately, whatever is said will be taken out of its proper context and put into a different context to fit whatever narrative it needs to fit to get ratings. Good ratings mean money.

As for sponsors, they can forget about those. CenturyLink dropped Denver Broncos linebacker Brandon Marshall as a company spokesman almost immediately after he protested during the anthem. It takes real *cajones* for someone to sacrifice a paycheck for their beliefs. Standing for those beliefs - if they're genuine - is one of the most altruistic and noble things a person can do in life.

Another thing that happens to vocal Black celebrities is that everywhere they go, the only thing people want to talk about is what they said or did, and not why they said or did it. The media changes and controls the narrative. A good example in regards to the Kaepernick protest is the rarely talked about fact that an ex-Green Beret asked Kaepernick to kneel out of *respect* for the military (Kaepernick originally sat down during the anthem). Many media outlets and pundits who disagreed with his protest would say he hated the military. In the end, the plight of people of color in this country at the hands of law enforcement (the original message) is drowned out by the actions the messenger uses to get his message across.

Sound familiar?

It should if you read the New Testament.

And before anyone gets their panties in a bunch about that sentence, I will not apologize and I stand by its biblical accuracy.

In other words: *I said what the fuck I said.*

Even *after* Black celebrities put their boots on the ground and put their money where their mouth is, there are still going to be pundits claiming it was a P.R. stunt; even after the Black celebrity lost money, friends, and connections because they decided to stand on their morals. These are the same morals that run counter to unchecked capitalism, blatant systemic racism, and educational and economic oppression of people of color in the United States.

If I was to become famous and knew that I could risk everything I gained by speaking up for marginalized and vulnerable people, I would still stand up for what's right and speak my truth. If it costs me money, friendships, and anything else fame entails, then I take it as a sign from the Universe that "all that glitters ain't gold.

Fuck it.

If my opinion costs me potential readers, *I'm okay with that as well.* I'm not for everyone and that's another reason I don't care if I become famous or not.

Computer Love

College journalist Brian, 2007.

Before Facebook and Myspace, there was BlackPlanet.com.

I LOVED BlackPlanet! It was the spot to be when trying your hand at computer love. I was online communicating with whichever woman was receptive to my advances. I even met a few nice girls.

I met "Denise" on BlackPlanet. Denise was so damn fine in her profile picture that I felt like I'd be doing myself a disservice if I didn't at least attempt to get her phone number. So I started instant messaging her, trying to get to know her while trying to get her number. After about a month (*THE* longest month of my young life), I finally got it.

What took her so fucking long?

We started talking over the phone and one day I asked to take her to a movie. She said sure.

In my brain, I'm thinking, "*She wants the D!*"

So we planned the date. For the sake of recognition, I asked her what she would be wearing. She said tight blue jeans, black shoes, and a *Nautica* brand jacket. *Nautica* went out of style in the seventh grade and I was every bit of seventeen, so that should have raised a red flag. Red flags be damned, I was a horny and desperate teenage virgin.

I'm a horny, desperate thirty-plus year old man - some things never change.

Anyway, I told her I would be wearing a black *Carhartt* jacket and all black everything else.

What could I say? I look great in black.

The day of the date came and I was kind of nervous, so I asked my homies to come with me to the movie theater where I was supposed to meet Denise. I called her from my cell phone - a black Motorola flip phone, stylish at the time - to ask her where she was. She said she was on the third floor. I went up the escalator.

I bullshit you not: at the top of the escalator I saw the *Nautica* jacket, the tight blue jeans, and black shoes...

... but that wasn't the "Denise" I was expecting.

This grown-ass woman was almost fifty years old! I was only *seventeen!* She reminded me of a Black version of the bird lady in Central Park from *Home Alone 2: Lost In New York!*

I turned around and ran down the escalator.

My homies - who were on the second floor - saw me running down the escalator and asked me, "Yoooooo, what's up?"

I yelled at them, "Let's fucking go! Let's get out of here before 'The Bird Lady' comes and gets me!" I was a bit overdramatic, but it worked.

We got to the parking garage and my phone rang. HOLY SHIT - IT WAS THE BIRD LADY! I picked up the phone and she asked me, "Why did you run?"

Being a *terrible* liar, I told her, "That was my brother. I had him see if you were at the theatre yet. I'm in the parking garage. I'll be up once I park." She knew it was a lie because she could hear me driving that stolen Cutlass Supreme I had back into the bustling 27th street traffic.

I was gone.

She called my phone over twenty times after that incident before I finally told her, "Lady, nothing is going to happen with us *whatsoever* because you're older than my mother - and my mom is *old*. We can still be friends on BlackPlanet." I told her that "we can still be friends on BlackPlanet" lie while intending to block her.

She was creepy as hell.

From that point on, I stopped meeting up with girls from the internet... until I discovered Myspace. I really fucked up on

Myspace, buddy.

I guess some things never change.

Brian's Dream Girl

Drinking the troubles away Brian, 2015.

The year was 2007 and I was a college freshman five years after my high school graduation. I waited five years to pursue higher education because I needed a break; I've been in school since I was four years old! Also around that time in my life, I was a knucklehead who was ripping and running the streets doing "wild nigga shit." I couldn't juggle that lifestyle with working forty hours a week and going to school full time; so I chose the streets over school. Once the streets chewed me up and spat me out, I decided to go to college.

In hindsight, it was a terrible idea to go to school full time and work full time, but that's not what this story is about. I jumped headfirst into school because I figured I was smart enough to handle it, which I was. Yet, I was habitually tired due to my 40-hour work weeks.

"Running on fumes" became my life because I crammed studying and homework into every idle moment I had; work breaks, before and after school, before and after work, in between classes. As a result, I got roughly four hours of sleep per night. I called myself *"cutting myself a break"* because sixty percent of my classes were mostly reading and writing, things I could do in my sleep.

The other forty percent *LITERALLY* caused me to lose sleep: psychology and math. I hated those classes so much, they haunted me in my dreams.

One night, I had a crazy, college- related dream. The thing that stuck out the most in the midst of the chaotic dream was this girl. She was fucking *GORGEOUS!*

She had this beautiful dark chocolate skin that practically *glowed!* She had long and curly natural hair, a perfect smile, a short stature, and petite frame. I never saw a woman that beautiful in real life! I was in that dream fighting off *math test-wielding dragons* and a Nubian goddess is in the midst of it all - calm and serene.

I woke up thinking, "Yo! What the fuck was *THAT* about?!" Until that time, I've never dreamt with that much detail about someone I've never seen or met! I've fought **dragons, leprechauns, mercenaries, leprechaun mercenaries on dragons,** and all types of crazy shit in my dreams before but WHO WAS THAT LADY?! I felt like I woke up in love with a complete stranger! I couldn't shake the feeling!

Weeks went by and I'm still in school and still not sleeping. As a result, my productivity nosedived. I went from a B in math to a D and in psychology, I went from a C to a big-ass F! I *completely* tanked the midterm in my psychology class, so I sought out the professor to see if there was any way to improve my grade.

I ran into the professor in the hallway after class and talked to him about the midterm. We're in the midst of this conversation when I get the feeling I'm being watched. I turned around and lo and behold, *THERE STOOD MY DREAM GIRL!*

She looked exactly how she looked in my dream! The hair, smile, frame, calming presence; I dreamt of this woman! Now there she was - close enough to see my heart beating out of my chest while smiling deep into my soul! And I said ABSOLUTELY NOTHING! I was speechless for once.

I was stuck in the gaze of the woman I had only dreamed about; the psych professor's words went from English to the sound of Charlie Brown's teacher in the background. When I was staring into her honey brown eyes, I could have sworn I heard angels singing "I Do Love You" by the soul group GQ. I'm almost sure that my heart was a few BPMs away from exploding and I was maybe five seconds away from creaming my underwear, dude. It was *surreal.*

So surreal that *I panicked and walked away* mid-conversation with the psychology professor who I immediately ignored once I caught a glimpse of my dream girl. I had to shake the spot immediately; I couldn't risk fainting in the presence of either person.

Later that day, I was at my second job as the groundskeeper at the college I was attending. It was about 1:30 in the afternoon, several hours after I bitched up when I saw my dream girl, and I was *still* shaken up. My coworkers were saying things like, "Brian looks like he saw a ghost because I've *NEVER* seen a pale, dark-skinned Black dude!" They didn't even give me an assignment list; they just let me wander aimlessly around the campus in a golf cart.

"Brian's gonna Brian," I guess.

As I was leaving from the student parking garage, I heard an unfamiliar voice call my name. I know I've never heard the voice before, but I got an erection *IMMEDIATELY!* I knew it was the angelic dream girl! My mind began to race, my heart started beating too fast, and I was covered in sweat in seconds!

I saw her crossing the street going towards the parking garage and I began to steer the golf cart in her direction. I got four or five feet away from her and she was smiling from ear to ear!

WHAT THE FUCK IS GOING ON?!

I asked her the first question on my mind.

"How do you know *MY* name?"

She began to laugh. It was *the most beautiful laugh I had ever heard*; it was like baby angels laughing at the world's greatest memes. I'm sure that when God made this woman, He walked around heaven high-fiving angels, saying, *"Yeah, dawg, I killed the game with this one!"*

She said to me, "Brian, I sit two seats behind you in psychology. You always smell like weed and you're always laughing at inappropriate shit."

I thought to myself, *"Brian to Ground Control, Brian to Ground*

Control - PREPARE TO CREAM YOUR UNDERWEAR!"

Now if you're keeping score at home, not only did she know my name, but we had a class together, she knew I love to smoke weed, and she knew my corny ass liked to laugh at *ALL* the inappropriate shit!

Where did this woman come from if not straight from The Good Lord Almighty's bosom?

I was flabbergasted! The only thing I could muster up was a blank stare.

Brian, you're being a little bitch right now.

We finished making small talk - well not "we" because *she* talked and I just sat there smiling like a *fucking goober* the entire time - and we went our separate ways after telling each other we would talk later. I was in the middle of the street in a golf cart, momentarily paralyzed! My dream girl not only knew I existed, she *talked to me* and told me that we were going to *talk again!*

WHAT IN THE WORLD WAS GOING ON?

Some days passed and we kept our promise of talking to one another in passing. She would see me doing my groundskeeping duties and stop to chat for a while. That was usually the highlight of my day. Unfortunately, it didn't negate the fact that I was *still* failing psychology.

In an effort to save my GPA, I withdrew from psychology and took a "W" instead of an "F." Cool, no major dent in my GPA. The adverse effect of dropping psych was that *my dream girl disappeared*! Vanished! I didn't see her around campus anymore nor did I see her in the psychology class we used to share when I would decide to peek in occasionally.

I felt defeated.

I literally met *THE WOMAN OF MY DREAMS*, spoke with

her multiple times, *and didn't get her name or phone number!* I felt like the biggest idiot on the planet!

Even now, many years later, I still kick myself for not getting her name, number, social media information or *anything.* How could you be so stupid, Brian?

I finally understand that Teddy Pendergrass song, "The Whole Town (Is Laughing At Me)."

Brian, you're a little bitch.

Skankin' It Up For Nuggets

Chef Brian, 2020.

My first full time job was as a night cook at a burger joint. I was sixteen years old, on probation, I was a *major* pothead, and an honor roll student who worked a little over forty-five hours a week, all rolled into one.

I was also a virgin.

In my neighborhood, all of my homies would brag about their sexual conquests and all I would do was sit and listen. It would *ALWAYS* go from the homies talking about having sex to the homies talking about me *not* having sex.

I'd hope they would spare me the bullshit, so I'd blurt out, "But this girl let me suck her boobs!"

They would reply, "Nah, cuzz, you've never felt no *PUSSY*! You haven't even put a finger in one!"

It was true: not even a *finger.* In my defense, I'm somewhat of a germaphobe. I'm also extremely shy and socially awkward. Super awkward.

Even worse, I caught hell at work about my virginity, too!

If you have *never* worked in a kitchen, you'll never understand how profane, vulgar, ornery, inappropriate, and downright nasty a kitchen crew can be. I'm pretty sure I swear more in a kitchen than anywhere else, and I swear all the time. Kitchens are where dick jokes have a longer shelf life than the majority of the inventory. It's not the place for someone with tender ears or a person who lacks a dark sense of humor.

Anyway, one of my best friends and favorite coworker, Gijuan, gave me *the* most shit about being a virgin.

"Damn, B - when are you gonna do something about your *situation*?" he asked me one day.

"What situation, Gijuan?"

"THAT DRY ASS DICK, NIGGA! Go get some pussy, even if you have to pay for it!"

"I'm not paying for pussy, cuzz. No sir!"

"Brian, everybody pays for pussy, directly or indirectly. Trust me."

(That was the best advice about sex/relationships that I've ever

received, by the way.)

Those conversations happened every shift. I started to think, "I need to get laid and get this shit over with!"

Here's the thing, though: I never really concerned myself with losing my virginity because of two reasons - I never had any free time and I was *DEATHLY* afraid of my mother!

My mother always said, "Don't be out there fucking with those little fast-ass girls and think you're going to bring nappy-headed grandkids in here for me to babysit! You better wrap that shit up or move the fuck out!" I wasn't trying to move out over some pussy, bro. Y'all never had my mom's fried chicken; pussy can wait! Besides, I knew absolutely *NOTHING* about sex aside from innuendo and what the homies talked about. I was probably still scared of catching cooties, if we're going to be honest.

I would flirt with servers at my job almost religiously and nothing would come from it aside from a few boob touches and a nipple twist or two. The servers were all around my age, too, but they've all had sex before. I was the odd man out.

One night when we were closing up, I asked the servers to tell me what they wanted to eat. They were supposed to ring it up and pay half price, but I have no shame in saying that policy sucks. I gave the servers free food because I ate for free every twenty minutes or so during my shift; fuck this food, fam. Anyway, I got started cooking the food for the servers when The New Chick walked in the kitchen and asked for food.

I ask her, "What do you wanna eat?"

"I just want some nuggets."

"How many?"

"Surprise me," she said with a smile.

Now here is where I tell you that The New Chick had a nice

47

ass. She was a terrible server - *AN ABSOLUTE DUMPSTER FIRE* – but she had a nice ass and she smelled great. So I put some nuggets in the fryer for her.

I started wrapping the burgers and all the other food, writing on my coworkers' wrappers things like, "I hope you choke," "This sandwich was your nasty ass idea," "You gonna have diarrhea," and all kinds of shit because that's how degenerate kitchen guys operate. So when I got to The New Chick's order, I wrote on her box, "You owe me $$$" and slid the box through the expo window.

Why did she slide the box back with "What do I owe you?" followed by x's and o's.

I was clueless and I almost wrote, "Didn't your dumb ass see the dollar signs on the box?" My boy Gijuan said, "Look here, stupid; shorty trying to throw you some pussy!" During the entire conversation, The New Chick was in the expo window smiling at me.

I slid her food back to her without a response. I continued to do my job, trying to close the kitchen so I can go home and smoke some weed. I went to take the trash out and was cornered by The New Chick.

She pushed me against a wall and with a black Sharpie, she proceeded to write her phone number in the palm of my hand. "Make sure you call me!" she demanded.

"Ok."

"Do you even know my name?"

"Ummm… no."

"My name is The New Chick." *(Obviously that's not her name, but you get the picture.)*

I took the trash out and went back to the kitchen to write the number on a piece of paper so I could wash my hands. Gijuan saw what I was doing and yelled to the entire kitchen, "Looks like our boy is about to be a man, y'all! He got the digits!"

Everybody in the kitchen went crazy; clapping and congratulating me like I discovered the cure for cancer or something! I was just sitting there looking stupid. I wasn't sure I was going to call.

I forgot her name and she didn't write it down in the palm of my hand.

Two days later, I was at work and The New Chick stormed into the kitchen, pushed me up against the walk-in cooler door and yelled at me, "You haven't called me?! Why?! Do you have a girlfriend?!"

"Nah, just been busy. Work and school."

"Well since you're obviously bullshitting, there's no school Friday. I checked the schedule and you don't work Friday. So here's my address. Come over on Friday!" She handed me a piece of paper with her address on it.

"Come over for what?" I asked. "Are you trying to smoke?"

"BOY, YOU BETTER BRING YOUR ASS OVER ON FRIDAY!"

I'm not gonna lie: I was low-key scared. It was obvious she was aggressive as hell! I asked myself if I needed to go to her house with my pistol or not. The New Chick was fucking crazy!

"I'll see you Friday," I reluctantly replied.

She walked off. Gijuan popped up out of nowhere like the virginity genie that doesn't grant wishes, yelling out "MY BOY FINNA GET HIS DICK WET!" loud enough for the general manager to hear.

"Are you talking about Brian?" the general manager asked Gijuan. "If so, It's about damn time!"

I never liked the general manager.

Friday came and I was nervous as hell. I don't know what

49

the fuck I was doing! I was shy as hell and had no idea how to initiate sex, as evidenced by my virginity. I was scared. I smoked about a half ounce of weed before I even left my mom's house!

I went to The New Chick's house, armed with a bottle of Seagram's gin and three blunts rolled up. I was still super nervous because I really didn't know this girl. I knocked a few times and while I was waiting, I took a huge shot of gin. The burning of my throat caused me to frown up.

She answered the door in a gray shirt and black sweats and asked me, "What the hell is wrong with you?"

As I passed her the bottle, I mouthed,"This shit is *nasty!*"

I walked in the house and the entire house is *covered* in plastic. This had to be her grandma's house or her mom was just old as hell. She led me to her bedroom and almost immediately. I started sweating.

I took a seat on her bed and started rubbing my sweat-drenched hands against my thighs (something I still do when nervous). She was in the midst of cleaning a CD with rubbing alcohol when she accidentally (on purpose) spilled the entire bottle on her shirt.

"Guess I have to take her shirt off," she seductively said.

Before I could register what was going on, she was naked and taking my belt off.

"Oh shit Brian, it's really happening," I said to myself.

She got on top of me and as soon as it began, it ended. I probably came in four minutes or so. I went to the restroom, disposed of the condom in the toilet, and used *SOMEBODY'S* face towel to clean myself up. I was ready to leave. I got what I came for.

The next day, I got to work and the entire night crew - servers included - were congratulating me like I just won the Super Bowl. I was confused - I didn't tell anyone about losing my virginity, not even the homies!

Almost as if she was reading my mind, The New Chick popped up like, "I told our coworkers that I took your virginity. They're really proud of you."

"Why?"

"So they won't call you 'Desert Dick Brian' anymore."

"They call me that?"

"You're welcome. I also told them that you're my boyfriend now."

Well, once the shift ended, Gijuan and the guys bought me drinks to congratulate me on losing my virginity. I was distracted all night. How dare The New Chick declare me her boyfriend without my permission? What the fuck was going on?

How do I get out of this mess?

To be continued...

Sketchy Nerd Homies

Arizona Brian, 2015.

The year was 2008 and I was living in Tucson, Arizona. At the time, I was working in this call center for a very well-known cable company who I won't name because I'm not petty.

While working for the unnamed company, I would disguise my voice and answer the phone with a Middle Eastern accent - just for laughs. Every now and then, someone would be super upset and demand to speak to a manager, so I'd tell them there was a thirty minute wait for a manager, and they'd be fine with waiting. In reality, management didn't want us escalating calls, so I would use that thirty minutes to go to my car and smoke a joint and take tequila shots. I would get back on the call with my regular voice and pretend I'm my own manager. It was pretty hilarious to me.

During lunch break, I used to go around the corner from the job to smoke weed. There were usually about five to ten people already there, getting baked, and everybody was pretty cool and got along just fine. That's where I met this dude named Ryan.

Ryan was chill. We both liked tequila and we both listened to Tech N9ne's music. We became friends pretty quickly. He eventually started paying me gas money to take him to and from work, which was pretty cool because extra money is fine with me.

I started to hang out with Ryan after work. We would meet at the park by his house to smoke, listen to music, and crack jokes and shit. One day, he said to me, "Hey bro, you gotta come over to my house and play the game with me and my roommates!"

I was down.

We got to Ryan's apartment and the first thing I noticed were the computers. There were three computers in the living room with multiple screens. I'm thinking to myself, "So this mothafucka running a call center in his home while working for one? What kind of corporate espionage bullshit is he mixed up with?" The computers struck me as strange until I surveyed the rest of the living room.

These mothafuckas had at least twenty swords. Swords, amigo. Not only swords, but ancient kinds of swords! *THESE MOTHAFUCKAS HAD ROMAN BROADSWORDS AND SHIT!* It was borderline creepy as fuck.

I sat on the couch and grabbed an Xbox controller while Ryan and his two roommates proceeded to take seats at their computers. I asked them, "So none of y'all want y'all asses kicked on *Madden*? I thought we were playing video games!"

"We are, but the game is on the computer," Ryan tells me. "You've never heard of *World of Warcraft?*"

Those dudes spent *hours* on *World of Warcraft*, yelling at each other and into their headsets. I didn't mind because I would drink and play *Madden* alone, randomly yelling at my offensive line to *"please just fucking block somebody for the love of God!"*

A few months go by of us hanging out and shit when one day Ryan calls me and says, "Hey, there's this new shit for *World of Warcraft* that's being released at midnight at GameStop. Do you think you could drop me and the guys off at eleven and pick us up around 1:30? I'll have gas money."

"Shit cuzz," I told him, "you had me at 'gas money'! I'll see y'all at 10:30."

I got to their house around 10:45 p.m. and sounded my horn. I didn't get out of the car because Jodeci was on the radio and I was in the car hitting those high notes, baby! *You know I'm an R&B superstar in the making!* I was so busy singing that I paid little attention to these three nerds getting in my car with huge backpacks. I was just waiting on Ryan to drop them coins in my hand for gas money. Once I got the cash, I pulled off and headed to GameStop.

I got to GameStop and I couldn't believe my eyes! There were maybe a hundred people in the parking lot in costume! Wizards, witches, warlocks, elves, gnomes, leprechauns, all kinds of mythical creatures were present and accounted for. A light bulb went off in my head and I addressed the elephant in the car.

I asked them, "There's costumes in those bags, huh?"

These three goobers started laughing until I interrupted their laughter with some real shit.

I told them:

"You guys are cool and all, but when I come to pick you guys up, you better have on regular clothes! I'm not bullshitting, fellas. I'm not going to be riding around northwest Tucson at two in the morning with three white wizards and warlocks and shit in an Oldsmobile that smells like weed!

Apparently, they weren't receptive to my message because when I came back to get them, I saw three wizards on the curb. I kept driving. I called Ryan and said, "Y'all better change or get a cab, dawg! I'm not playing about those costumes.

Ryan called a cab.

I picked him up from his house for work later in the week and there were no hard feelings. He told me it was actually pretty funny because he didn't think I would leave without them. When it became apparent I was serious, they started laughing and told the other wizards and warlocks and shit the entire "Brian ain't riding in an Oldsmobile that smells like weed with three white wizards" story and they all got a good laugh out of it.

We would lose touch after I quit the call center, but anytime I see a GameStop, I always think about the sketchy nerd homies.

Monkey-Slapped

Monkey I stayed away from, 2015.

So **BOOM**: here I am at Nairobi National Park. It's ridiculously beautiful, right? Ridiculously fucking beautiful. The weather's absolutely perfect, the animals were cool, I'm a wee bit hungover, the scene was practically majestic.

These little monkeys were just running around and shit and I steered clear of them. Little or not - they're *wild fucking animals* IN AFRICA!

There were a TON of kindergarten-aged kids (henceforth

referred to by their scientific name, "*little baby people*") in their little school uniforms, having little baby people conversations. You could tell the little baby people were all from different schools by their different uniforms. They were running all over the park pointing and talking shit about animals and doing whatever little baby people do.

I happened to look over to my right and I saw a little baby person and a little baby monkey in the midst of a relatively heated altercation. The baby monkey *slapped* the little baby person! Before I could even start laughing, the little baby person *MACK DADDY PIMP SLAPPED THE SHIT* out of the little baby monkey dude!

I could tell that the little baby monkey dude was embarrassed because he got pimp-slapped in front of his little baby monkey homies and the little baby monkey women - and we all know how little baby monkey women gossip!

So that's the story of that one time I saw a little baby person pimp-slap a monkey while I was in Kenya.

Karibu sana.

(That's Swahili for "You're welcome.")

Engine in the Front Seat

My best friend Darryl and I, 2019.

Let me begin by saying that this story is very difficult for me to tell, even though it happened a few years ago.

If you know me, you know that I'm rarely speechless and I can talk your ear off. Yet, what happened on Labor Day 2018 left me completely speechless, and if we're being honest, a wee bit traumatized.

"A wee bit" is a lie. I'm still pretty fucked up about it.

My then-girlfriend "Charli" and I were at a close friend's house, enjoying the Labor Day holiday festivities. Cold drinks were available, we had good weed in the air, we were listening to some outstanding music, we played cards and shit; it was a great day.

When it started to get late, my best friend Darryl and his wife decided they were going to go home. Charli and I decided to follow them to their house and continue to party; it's not like I had to work the next day. So we hopped in my van and followed Darryl to his house.

It was approximately two am and it was pitch dark on the highway. We traveled four miles or so before I made out a shadow under an overpass at the last minute. Darryl, who was ahead of me, swerved around the shadow. I swerved around and stopped immediately, honking my horn repeatedly for Darryl to stop. What I saw was horrifying.

In the middle of the highway was an early-2000 Chevrolet Suburban. It was facing east and west, taking up all 3 lanes on a northbound highway. *Every airbag in the vehicle was deployed!* The front end was so damaged, the engine was in the front seat!

The engine was in the front seat, *so where the hell was the driver?*

The driver was in the middle lane of the highway, with his body facing southbound, sitting with his legs crossed, *COVERED IN BLOOD* in front of his wide open driver side door.

I turned my hazard lights on and got out of the van. I told Darryl, "Bro, we have to help this man before he gets killed!"

There was no light under the overpass. Darryl and I had to drive on the shoulder of the road to avoid colliding with the Suburban, something a semi truck would be unable to do at sixty miles per hour. I asked Charli and Darryl's wife Veronica to watch our backs so Darryl and I wouldn't get hit attempting to get the blood-soaked man out of the middle of the highway.

We approached the man and the only thing I can remember in regards to his appearance was that he was a bloody, older Black man. All I really remember seeing was blood. I asked him if he could move on his own and he told me he couldn't.

Around that time, other cars began to come around the curve, barely missing the Suburban, my van, Darryl's car, and us. Veronica and Charli were a hundred yards or so ahead of us, trying to signal for cars to go around us. A few cars stopped and turned their hazard lights on to warn other cars, but there were still a lot of cars driving past us.

I called 911 and I can never forget this phone call because I had the *WORST DISPATCHER IN AMERICA!* Thinking about that phone call gets me upset all over again.

I'm not going to lie; I was fucking hysterical! I was scared someone was going to kill the man because they wouldn't be able to see him while they're coming around a small turn at over sixty miles per hour. I told the dispatcher, "Ma'am, we need help immediately! There was a man who was in a bad accident on 71 highway and he's in the middle lane covered in blood! We need all the emergency personnel we can get! There's fucking cars speeding by us and I fear its going to get ugly!"

The dispatcher had the audacity to tell me, *"Watch your language and calm down!"*

I COULDN'T REMEMBER THE LAST TIME I HAD BEEN THAT ANGRY!

I responded, "Look, **BITCH**! There is a man covered in blood in the middle lane of the fucking highway and he's going to fucking get hit by a car if you don't send a fucking ambulance and the fucking police! Why are you worried about my fucking language?"

I hung up the phone and asked Charli to call 911 because I was not only hysterical, freaking out, and downright scared for all of our safety, but I was angry that someone had the nerve to tell me to watch my language while I'm attempting to get a man to safety. I can't think straight when I'm angry.

Instead of waiting on the ambulance, I told Darryl, "Hey bro, we're going to have to get him out of the street ourselves!"

Darryl grabbed the man's arms, I grabbed his legs, and adrenaline helped us get him to the shoulder of the highway by our cars. He was super fucking heavy!

Immediately after moving him out of harm's way to the shoulder of the road, a young blonde lady in scrubs, fresh from her shift at Truman Medical Center approached us and said, "Let me help you help him."

I said, "Please do; you're the professional." I was shaking like a leaf, trying to process what the fuck just happened.

After what seemed like an eternity (because I chain smoked about half a pack of cigarettes), the paramedics arrived and attempted to place the man on the gurney. They were having trouble lifting him from the ground. I was still pissed about the 911 dispatcher and what I considered a terrible response time to a potentially tragic situation, so I angrily walked over and grabbed part of the spinal board with one hand while the four first responders were struggling to lift. With the adrenaline running through my body, the board *jumped* off the ground and I was able to help the paramedics load the man into the ambulance with no difficulty.

The other people that stopped along with the police kept talking to Darryl and I, calling us "brave," but I didn't pay much attention. My mind was somewhere else.

Dude, somebody was in the vehicle with that man and *left him to fucking die* in the middle of a highway. There is *NO WAY* that he could've got out of that SUV by himself with every airbag deployed *and the engine in the driver's seat!*

We eventually continued our journey to Darryl's house, riding silently in the early morning hours along a highway that was recently marred by a horrific accident. Charli spent the entire ride consoling me because I couldn't stop thinking about how that man couldn't have got out of the truck by himself; it was impossible! All the airbags were deployed; there had to be other people in the car.

"The engine was in the front seat. Somebody left him there to die," I repeated for over an hour.

The mood to party was ruined. Darryl, Veronica, and Charli all went to sleep immediately. I didn't sleep at all; I stayed up until I saw the sun, trying to drink the images in my head away.

To this day, I wonder what happened to that man. He told the nurse who stopped and assisted us that night that he was drunk driving. I still wonder how fast he was going to cause his engine to be in the front seat! I also wonder who got him out of the car and why they left him in the middle of the middle of the highway *to die!*

That's what bothered, and still bothers me the most about the situation: Somebody left that man in a compromising position. What kind of person would do that?

How many people passed that man up before Darryl and I decided to stop? How could you see someone in that situation and not stop to help a fellow human being? *What the fuck is wrong with people?*

* * *

Writing this story made me realize that I haven't completely shaken that night from my head. Maybe because I have way too many questions that I'll never be able to answer. Lord willing, the man learned a valuable lesson about the dangers of driving drunk. It almost cost him his life. Hell, it almost cost Darryl and I *our* lives trying to move him out of the street.

I still can't believe that shit happened. Somebody left that man in the middle of the highway with a Chevrolet Suburban engine in the driver's seat.

About the Author

Brian Gitachu is a songwriter, blogger, and journalist from Kansas City, Missouri. In his spare time, he enjoys eating cheeseburgers, cracking inappropriate jokes, and posting memes that gets him kicked off of social media for thirty days at a time.

You can connect with me on:

 https://briangitachu.medium.com

 https://twitter.com/BGitachu

 https://www.facebook.com/BGitachu